Saudi Arabian Heritage

Celebrating Diversity in My Classroom

I0886629

By Tamra B. Orr

21st Century Junior Library

Published in the United States of America by
Cherry Lake Publishing
Ann Arbor, Michigan
www.cherrylakepublishing.com

Reading Adviser: Cecilia Minden, PhD, Literacy expert and children's author

Photo Credits: ©hikrcn/Shutterstock, cover; ©mohamed hashif/Shutterstock, 4; ©HansMusa/Shutterstock, 6; ©Dragon Images/Shutterstock, 8; ©ZouZou/Shutterstock, 10; ©michaeljung/Shutterstock, 12; ©BestPhotoStudio/Shutterstock, 14; ©Anna_Pustynnikova/Shutterstock, 16; ©oneinchpunch/Shutterstock, 18; ©Omer Hindawi/Shutterstock, 20

Copyright ©2019 by Cherry Lake Publishing. All rights reserved. No part of this book may be reproduced or utilized in any form or by any means without written permission from the publisher.

Library of Congress Cataloging-in-Publication Data
Name: Orr, Tamra, author.
Title: Saudi Arabian heritage / by Tamra B. Orr.
Description: Ann Arbor : Cherry Lake Publishing, 2018. | Series: Celebrating diversity in my classroom | Includes bibliographical references and index.
Identifiers: LCCN 2018003270 | ISBN 9781534129030 (hardcover) | ISBN 9781534132238 (pbk.) | ISBN 9781534130739 (pdf) | ISBN 9781534133938 (hosted ebook)
Subjects: LCSH: Saudi Arabia—Juvenile literature. | Saudi Arabia—Social life and customs—Juvenile literature.
Classification: LCC DS204.25 .O77 2018 | DDC 953.8—dc23
LC record available at https://lccn.loc.gov/2018003270

Cherry Lake Publishing would like to acknowledge the work of the Partnership for 21st Century Skills. Please visit *www.p21.org* for more information.

Printed in the United States of America
Corporate Graphics

CONTENTS

Near the city of Al Ula, one can find the Elephant Rock Formation.

Sandy Saudi Arabia

Saudi Arabia is in the Middle East. It is 830,000 square miles (2.1 million square kilometers) in size. That is about one-fifth the size of the United States. Twenty-eight million people live there. Most people live in the big cities. That's because 95 percent of the country's area is hot and dry deserts.

It is not unusual for Saudis to **immigrate** to the United States. That number skyrocketed between 2010 and 2014. Let's explore their homeland.

Riyadh is the capital city of Saudi Arabia.
It also has the highest population.

Ahlan wa Sahlan

Almost everyone throughout the Middle East speaks Arabic. **Dialects** sometimes change from one country to another. When Arabic words are written, they look like art. *"Ahlan wa Sahlan"* means "Welcome" in Arabic. It is written أهلا وسهلا.

Many people in the biggest cities of Saudi Arabia also speak English. It is taught in most private and public schools. Another language

Many people from the Philippines move to Saudi Arabia for work.

found in Saudi Arabia is Tagalog, It was brought by people from the Philippines who immigrated there. “Welcome” in Tagalog is *“Maligayang Pagdating.”*

Think!

Saudi Arabia’s Ghawar Field is the world’s largest oil field. It has produced about 75 billion barrels of oil. That would fill 4.8 million Olympic-size swimming pools! The world depends on Saudi Arabia’s huge oil reserves. What do countries need it for? How does that affect the country?

The Kaaba is a building in the middle of Islam's most sacred mosque. Many people come here to pray.

A Shared Belief

All Saudis are Muslim. They follow the religion of Islam. By law, all citizens must be Muslim. People who follow other faiths have sometimes been arrested and put in prison.

The country's system of laws is based on religious rules. Some of these rules decide how people should dress. Both men and women wear clothing covering their entire bodies. That includes their heads. They do this to express **modesty**. Women wear a

Saudis cover their bodies, but they wear light fabrics so they don't get hot.

niqab, a cloth covering their faces except for their eyes. They also wear an *abaya*. This is a long, black coat that is loose fitting. It covers everything except their hands and face. Men wear a *thobe*, an ankle-length piece of clothing with long sleeves. On their heads, they wear a white hat and a large square cloth. A black cord holds the cloth in place.

Saudi children start school at age 6. Boys and girls are taught in separate classes. Almost everyone knows how to read and write. About 80 percent of young men have jobs. But less than half of young women do.

Kebabs originated in Persia and Turkey.
Today they are eaten all over the world.

Kebabs and Pita

Do you like the same food as your parents and grandparents? If you lived in Saudi Arabia, you probably would. They have been eating the same foods for generations.

Muslims eat a lot of lamb and chicken. Beef is rarely eaten. Cubes of meat slid onto wooden sticks and grilled with vegetables are *kebabs*. Almost all meals are served with *pita*, a flat bread. Pita is often served with

Hummus is very healthy. It has protein, fiber, and vitamins.

hummus, a dip made out of chickpeas. Lentil soup is a popular side dish.

Religion guides some food choices in Saudi Arabia. Muslims are not allowed to eat pork or drink alcohol. On some holidays, they are required to **fast** from sunrise to sunset.

Coffee is served just a little bit at a time. The guest must tell the server if they don't want any more.

Coffee and Changes

Most Saudis will happily welcome you into their homes. This is true whether you are a friend, family, or a stranger. Many Saudis will light **incense** to show **hospitality**. Next, you will be offered hot, rich coffee. It is served in small cups, along with dates or other sweets.

Things are different in Saudi Arabia. In many public places, men and women are expected to stand in separate lines. This is true in

Women were permitted to drive in June 2018. Saudi leaders wanted to encourage women to be a part of the workforce.

banks and airports. But this is slowly changing. In 2018, women were given the right to drive. The country's Crown Prince Mohammed bin Salman lifted a driving **ban**. A month later, he declared women could attend sporting events in stadiums. But the women have to sit in a separate section. Change is slowly happening in the country.

Look!

Riyadh, Saudi Arabia's capital city, has a big camel market. About 100 camels are sold there daily. What might the camels be used for? Why would they be more helpful than other animals?

GLOSSARY

ban (BAN) an order forbidding something

dialects (DYE-uh-lekts) ways of speaking in particular areas

immigrate (IM-ih-grayte) to enter and settle in another country

fast (FAST) to not eat or drink anything

hospitality (hah-spih-TAL-ih-tee) kindness to visitors

incense (IN-sens) substance burned for its smell

modesty (MAH-dist-ee) shyness about your body

Arabic Words

abaya (uh-BAH-yah) a long black cloak that covers everything except for the hands and face

Ahlan wa Sahlan (EH-len WAH SEH-len) welcome

hummus (HUH-muss) a dip made out of chickpeas

kebabs (kuh-BAHBS) cubes of meat slid onto wooden sticks and cooked with vegetables

niqab (nih-KAHB) a cloth covering people's entire faces except for their eyes

pita (PEE-tuh) a thin, flat Middle Eastern bread that can hold meat, vegetables, or other fillings

thobe (THOBE) an ankle-length garment with long sleeves

Tagalog Words

Maligayang Pagdating (mah-li-GAH-yuhng PAHG-dah-ting) welcome

FIND OUT MORE

BOOKS

Cunnane, Kelly. *Deep in the Sahara.* New York: Schwartz and Wade Books, 2013.

Khan, Ausma Zehanat. *Ramadan: The Holy Month of Fasting.* Victoria, BC: Orca Book Publishers, 2018.

Khan, Hena. *Crescent Moons and Pointed Minarets: A Muslim Book of Shapes.* San Francisco: Chronicle Books, 2018.

WEBSITES

A to Z Kids Stuff—Saudi Arabia
www.atozkidsstuff.com/saudia.html
Find information about Saudi Arabia and lots of helpful links.

Ducksters—Saudi Arabia
www.ducksters.com/geography/country.php?country=Saudi%20Arabia
Learn quick facts about Saudi Arabia.

Easy Science for Kids—Saudi Arabia
http://easyscienceforkids.com/all-about-saudi-arabia/
Read fun facts about many aspects of Saudi Arabia.

INDEX

ABOUT THE AUTHOR

Tamra Orr is the author of hundreds of books for readers of all ages. She graduated from Ball State University, but moved with her husband and four children to Oregon in 2001. She is a full-time author, and when she isn't researching and writing books, she writes letters to friends all over the world. Orr enjoys life in the big city of Portland and feels very lucky to be surrounded by so much diversity.

21st Century **Junior** Library

The 21st Century Junior Library introduces young readers to important core content. Simple activities encourage students to **Look**, **Think**, **Make a Guess**, **Ask Questions**, and **Create**. The combination of reading and inquiring helps them develop the skills needed to master content and learn and succeed in the 21st century.

Read all of these 21st Century Junior Library titles to learn more about the diversity in your classroom:

Afghan Heritage
Chinese Heritage
Cuban Heritage
Dominican Heritage
Filipino Heritage
Indian Heritage
Korean Heritage
Mexican Heritage
Nepali Heritage
Saudi Arabian Heritage
Somali Heritage
Syrian Heritage
Venezuelan Heritage
Vietnamese Heritage

GR: P

ISBN-13: 978-1534132238

9 781534 132238

CHERRY LAKE Publishing

www.cherrylakepublishing.com

WELCOME TO THE CONSTRUCTION SITE

Bulldozer

Samantha Bell